FREDERICK DOUGLASS REPUBLICANS™

FREDERICK DOUGLASS REPUBLICANS

The Movement to Re-Ignite America's Passion for Liberty

K.CARL SMITH with Dr. Karnie C. Smith Sr

TO: KATIE

Live FREE !

K a Smith

authorHOUSE®

AuthorHouse™
1663 Liberty Drive
Bloomington, IN 47403
www.authorhouse.com
Phone: 1-800-839-8640

The ConservativeMESSENGER
PO Box 9402
Birmingham, AL 35220
www.conservativemessenger.org
Re-Igniting America's Passion for Liberty™

Follow us on:
FaceBook *- Frederick Douglass Republicans*
Twitter*: FDRepublicans*

First published by AuthorHouse 6/23/2011
ISBN: 978-1-4567-5814-1 (e)
ISBN: 978-1-4567-5815-8 (dj)
ISBN: 978-1-4567-5816-5 (sc)
Library of Congress Control Number: 2011905012
Printed in the United States of America

Any people depicted in stock imagery provided by Thinkstock are models, and such images are being used for illustrative purposes only.
Certain stock imagery © Thinkstock.

This book is printed on acid-free paper.

To the memory and courage of

FREDERICK DOUGLASS

A role model for Liberty, Politicians and the Next Generation

Acknowledgements!

To Jehovah God for giving me the strength to perform three roles: grandfather, father, and son—for I am a sinner saved by His grace.

My parents, Colonel (retired) Earnest C. and Bessie M. Smith, Sr. for their Christian example and committed faith. You are my superheroes. Thank you for giving me the wings to fly.

My children, Keith Carl-Marcus and Christie, thank you for believing in your dad.

My family members, Earnest Jr., Karnie Sr., Cydale, Kathy, Annette, Nikki, Samella, Earnest III, Karnie Jr., Camroyn, Karnell, Micah, Kennedy, Courtney and Kiley for all their love.

My brother, Dr. Karnie C. Smith, Sr. for his assistance with researching and taking my thoughts and putting them on paper—making them easily read and understood by anyone.

Former Arkansas Governor Michael Huckabee for encouraging me to write this book.

Lisa Hammond for her long-time support and prayers. Thank you for sharing a part of your life with me.

Vicky Brandy for her dedication and patience. While others doubted the message God has given me, you never waivered in your support. Thank you for being my political sounding board.

Yvonne Foreman, Derrick Frazier, Melissa Hudson, Beverly Jones, Lamar Lackey, Troy Towns, and Karl Washington for their friendship, encouragement and brutally honest feedback.

AuthorHouse Publishing for their professionalism and enthusiasm to partner with me in completing this project.

Faithful donors and volunteers who believe in what we do.

Alabama Federation of Republican Women, Alabama GOP, Conservative Patriots Club, Montgomery Tea Party Patriots, Rainy

Day Patriots Tea Party and Wetumpka Tea Party for their generous support.

All the members of the Frederick Douglass Republican Movement who champion liberty and the purpose of our cause. Together, we will improve the Republican Party and save our beloved nation.

LaSherril Brown Matthews, Joyce Bargeman and Rick Kiernan for their editing expertise and insightful suggestions.

To everyone who has prayed for my family and me. Thank you so very much.

- K. Carl Smith
The ConservativeMESSENGER™

PREFACE

The purpose of this book is to introduce the Frederick Douglass Republican Movement to the nation and to make public its principles. This is not an in-depth study on the philosophical views of Douglass. Instead, it is a tool for engagement—a powerful conservative-action handbook. It will enable closet conservatives to come out of the shadows and empower them to step into the arena of political debate, informed and confident.

This book provides Frederick Douglass Republicans with those skills and tools needed to engage at the local level—creating impact at the precinct and ultimately changing the political landscape of America.

This book provides hope to conservative Christians, who know they are not racists or Uncle Toms, but they are being unfairly mislabeled, misunderstood, and demonized—with the intent of silencing their voices. The answers and strategies you have long waited for are finally here.

In addition, this book is for those who have been masterfully deceived by the Democratic Party and unwittingly vote opposite their Christian values—knowing the truth will make you free.

Finally, this book is for future generations, encouraging them to become critical thinkers and active participants in the political process—agitators for their God-given right for self-rule.

The central theme that runs throughout this book is the commitment of Frederick Douglass Republicans to help today's Republican Party recapture its political distinction. To do so, Frederick Douglass Republicans will support only those politicians who make the plight of the poor a legislative priority—embracing Douglass' Life-Empowering Values: (1) Respect for the Constitution; (2) Respect for Life; (3) Belief in Limited Government, and (4) Belief in Personal Responsibility.

Anything less is unacceptable!

Knowing the facts enabled me to reach level #2—the ultimate goal. Without it, the goal of *"living by faith"* cannot be achieved.

To break the cycle of my *politico-schizophrenic* mindset required me to gather the facts about the issues, history and political platforms of each party. The only way to "build your faith" is by knowing and accepting the truth. I analyzed and evaluated those facts based on my Christian beliefs.

Finally, I developed a Political Value Structure for my life. The chapter entitled "A Final Word" includes an exercise that will help you establish your political values.

Level #2 – Living by Faith:

> [38] *Those who are right with me will live by faith. But if they turn back with fear, I will not be pleased with them.*
> - Hebrews 10:38 (NCV)

> [6] *And without faith it is impossible to please God, because anyone who comes to Him must believe that He exists and that He rewards those who earnestly seek Him.*
> - Hebrews 11:6 (NIV)

Facts produce faith. After developing my Political Value Structure, I had to decide if I would earnestly serve Jehovah God or if my ultimate allegiance would be to a political party.

Knowing my political values helped me make an educated and informed decision. As a result, I re-dedicated my life to Jesus Christ. Through the political party of my choice, I became actively involved in the legislative process to support the causes that lined up with my Christian values.

I promised God I would *"live by faith"* in all areas of my life, including politics.

Are You a Politico-Schizophrenic?

Why are you a Democrat? If you had asked me that question 15 years ago, my answer would have been something along these lines: *"I'm a Democrat because of my mother and father." "I'm a Democrat because it's a family tradition." "I'm a Democrat because I was born a Democrat." "I'm a Democrat because John F. Kennedy was a president for black folks." "I'm a*

Democrat for life so I will always vote Democrat." "I'm a Democrat because the Democratic Party is the party for the poor and the middle class." "I'm a Democrat because they supported the Civil Rights Movement." Finally, *"I'm a Democrat because that's all I know."*

My lack of knowing the true history of both parties (Republican and Democratic) twisted my whole outlook on politics. As a result, others easily persuaded me, and I fell for the deliberate schemes by Democratic politicians to deceive me.

My unwavering support for the Democratic Party overshadowed my allegiance to Jehovah God. Quick! Call 9-1-1 somebody. Some readers may be lapsing into a state of shock at this point. How can a Christian have unquestionable loyalty to a political party that campaigns on an anti-Christian platform?

The answer is simple. There were external forces influencing my emotions and decision-making when it came to politics. Allow me to explain.

Devious Manipulation of History

I know I was born black, but I also thought I was born a Democrat. But then one day I realized I was born neither a Democrat nor a Christian—I was born a sinner.

Just as I had to accept Christ for myself through studying and accepting His word as truth for me, I had to do the same with my political philosophy.

Once I embarked on the journey of reading my life backwards, my eyes were opened to the manipulative nature of images and how they influenced my thoughts, actions, feelings and political decision-making.

There is plenty of truth in the saying that a picture is worth a thousand words. As I looked back over my life, the Kennedy-King-Kennedy image led to my blind and total loyalty to the Democratic Party:

The Propaganda Portrait - The image of Dr. Martin Luther King, Jr., being flanked by President John F. Kennedy (JFK) and his brother Robert F. Kennedy (RFK) represents the biggest political lie that has ever

been told to black Americans. The Kennedy-King-Kennedy image was sold to black communities across the country beginning in the 1970s—a masterful propaganda campaign designed by the Democratic Party.

Obviously, this visual was designed to brainwash and mislead blacks. As a youth, I remember seeing this image on such items as throw rugs, ceramic plates, candlestick holders and church fans. In many black homes these items are considered heirlooms.

I have seen this print in many black households, prominently displayed near the Bible, the picture of the Last Supper or the family portrait.

In fact, as a teenager, I remember visiting a friend's home and saw one of these pictures hanging on the wall in the front room. While sitting there, his grandmother asked if I knew what these three men had in common. I told her I did not. She declared, *"The last name of each of these men ends in the letter 'K' and 'K' stands for kind."*

You will not find this portrait in the homes of younger blacks today. There is no need to—the propaganda is already deeply seated into their heads and hearts.

Similar to many blacks, through this image, I believed with all my heart that JFK and RFK were close members of my family. I was convinced they were supporters of Dr. King and champions for the Civil Rights Movement. The propaganda efforts of the Democratic Party had taken hold of my impressionable mind. The party that viciously exploited and enslaved my ancestors had masterfully deceived me to gain my vote and unquestionable loyalty. I have never been fooled like this before in all my life.

Unfortunately for Democrats, history tells a different story:

JFK on Civil Rights - President Dwight Eisenhower (a Republican) signed into law the Civil Rights Act of 1957. Primarily a voting rights bill, the 1957 Civil Rights Act was meant to ensure that all black Americans could exercise their right to vote. This was the first piece of civil rights legislation submitted to Congress since 1875 by President Ulysses S. Grant, another Republican president.[1]

The Civil Rights Act of 1957 was passed because it was a watered-down piece of legislation. The teeth that would have protected the voting rights of black Americans were removed. So how did the 1957 civil rights bill get weakened?

In its original draft was a condition that certain violations of it could be tried in court without the benefit of a *jury trial*. This was an important stipulation because history had shown that Southern juries would never convict a white person accused of violating the civil rights of a black person.

John Kennedy was a senator from the state of Massachusetts at the time. He supported the jury trial amendment that rendered the provisions of the 1957 civil rights bill virtually unenforceable. It passed by a vote of 51-42—a crushing blow to the Civil Rights Movement.[2]

Wiretaps on Dr. King - In 1961, Robert Kennedy, serving as his brother's U.S. Attorney General, authorized the FBI to wiretap Dr. King under the notion that communists were involved in the Civil Rights Movement. The surveillance continued for six years and no evidence of communist activities or influence was discovered.[3]

So, were the Kennedys champions of the Civil Rights Movement and supporters of Dr. King? Absolutely not! These facts of history are seldom discussed.

LBJ on Civil Rights - In the majority of history textbooks across the country, the second deceptive image that led to my *politico-schizophrenic* behavior was the photograph of President Lyndon B. Johnson signing the Civil Rights Act of 1964.

Just seven years earlier, while serving as the Democratic Senate Majority Leader, it was Lyndon B. Johnson who sent the 1957 civil rights bill to the judiciary committee. The racist senator who led the committee was Senator James Eastland from Mississippi. As a result, the bill was stripped of the provision protecting the voting rights of black Americans.[4]

LBJ picked up the civil rights bill introduced by President Kennedy. However, even though Democrats held almost two-thirds of the seats in Congress at that time, LBJ could not garner sufficient votes from within his own party to pass the bill. LBJ needed 269 votes from his party to achieve passage but could garner the support of only 198 of the 315 Democrats in Congress.

The 1965 Voting Rights Act by LBJ was a resurrection of Eisenhower's original language before it had been killed by Democrats. When it was finally approved under LBJ, of the 18 senators who opposed the Voting Rights Act, 17 were Democrats. In fact, 97 percent of Republican senators voted for the Act.[5]

So, did LBJ have a change of heart prior to signing the Civil Rights Act of 1964? Not hardly! In light of the national television broadcast of "Bull" Connor's brutal tactics against protest marchers in Birmingham, the federal government had to act quickly.

Fortunately for the Democratic Party, they were the ones occupying the White House and this gave them an excellent historical photo opportunity. What another masterful manipulation scheme by the Propaganda Party!

"Then you will know the truth, and the truth will set you free."
- John 8:32 (NIV)

Devious Manipulation of Language

The word "conservative" has a negative connotation within minority communities. If you call yourself a Black Conservative, Tea Party Conservative, Reagan Conservative, or a Christian Conservative, you might as well replace the word "conservative" with the word "racist" and identify yourself as a Black Racist, Tea Party Racist, Reagan Racist, or a Christian Racist. Why?

Remember the Democratic Party used the word "conservative". In the 1950s and 1960s, it was conservative Democrats who did everything possible to block civil rights legislation. They wanted to hold on to the principles of their "racist fathers" who produced Jim Crow Laws and the Black Codes.

The Republican Party also used the term "conservative". Unlike the Democratic Party, the Republican Party uses the word "conservative" to preserve the values of the "Founding Fathers" who wrote the Constitution and the Declaration of Independence—same word, but two entirely different meanings. I do not use the word conservative to describe myself politically. I am a Frederick Douglass Republican.

Tea Party Vindication
". . . You need firsthand evidence, not mere hearsay . . ."
2 Corinthians 13:5 (The Message)

11

Jesus ignored the negative public reports circulating in the community about Zacchaeus and dined with him to talk and share ideas until a real, authentic friendship was established (Luke 19:1-10). In a similar way, Douglass said on one occasion, *"I would unite with anybody to do right . . ."*[6]

Douglass' spirit of teamwork was evident in the Abolitionist Movement. He worked with Harriet Tubman, Harriet Beecher Stowe, Charles Sumner, Wendell Phillips and others. Like the Tea Party Movement, the Abolitionist Movement was made up of predominately white Americans.

Influenced by Jesus' friendship technique and Douglass' teamwork approach, I began attending many Tea Party meetings across the state of Alabama. In sharing ideas and making friends with thousands of Tea Party members, I discovered that the public perception of Tea Party activists as bigots and racists is not true. They are people who share Douglass' Life-Empowering Values.

The element of racism that may exist in the Tea Party Movement is nothing new. In fact, Douglass encountered racism within the predominately white Abolitionist Movement. For example, the Principal, Miss Tracy, expelled Douglass' daughter, Rosetta, from Seward Seminary in 1848. Miss Tracy was an active member of the Abolitionist Movement. Because of her abolitionist affiliation, Douglass assumed she would be fair and just; instead she was cruel and uncaring. Douglass was disappointed in the racist actions of his abolitionist friend, Miss Tracy. Douglass wrote:

> *"The principal -- after making suitable enquiries into the child's mental qualifications, and informing me of the price of tuition per term, agreed to receive the child into the school at the commencement of the September term. Here we parted. I went home, rejoicing that my child was about to enjoy advantages for improving her mind, and fitting her for a useful and honorable life. I supposed that the principal would be as good as her word -- and was more disposed to this belief, when I learned that she was an abolitionist -- a woman of religious principles and integrity -- and would be faithful in the performance of her promises, as she had been*

*prompt in making them. In all this I have been grievously
-- if not shamefully disappointed."*[7]

In spite of Miss Tracy's racist behavior, Douglass continued to fight for the freedom and progress of all Americans while reconciling and healing racial relations within the Abolitionist Movement.

Douglass impacted the lives of others in such a way that they went on to do great things: Abraham Lincoln emancipated the slaves; Charles Sumner founded the Republican Party; Mary White Ovington started the NAACP; and Booker T. Washington started Tuskegee Institute.

Last but not least, Douglass influenced Miss Tracy—Seward Seminary was integrated eight years later.

Likewise, Frederick Douglass Republicans are determined to create a similar impact within the Tea Party Movement and the Republican Party—interact and impact!

Obama-bashing is not my thing—in fact it is extremely counterproductive. Whenever I am invited to speak at Tea Party rallies, I make the following declaration, *"Drop the banners and pick up the Bible. Lay down your signs and raise the Constitution. This is not about getting laughs; it is about securing liberty and our God-given right for self-rule."*

The primary reason Tea Party activists are accused of racism and bigotry stems from the comic exaggerations of President Obama, portraying him as a monkey or the Joker. As we know and based on my personal knowledge, many of these offensive pictures of President Obama were stealthily placed at rallies to incriminate the Tea Party Movement.

Distasteful indeed, these depictions of President Obama are just as racist as the 2004 "Mammy" portrayal of Dr. Condoleezza Rice (who was then National Security Advisor to President George W. Bush) by the liberal Democrat and political cartoonist Jeff Danziger.[8]

Whether it is "Dr. Rice as Mammy" or "President Obama as a monkey or the Joker", they are both vile and obnoxious caricatures based on race—and not political satire.

If the caricatures of President Obama are what make Tea Party activists bigots and racists, then Jeff Danziger is also a bigot and a racist.

Black Democratic politicians, unelected black leaders and some of the most prominent black organizations are hypocrites of the highest order on this issue. They never came to Dr. Rice's defense, as one of their own (Jeff Danziger) depicted her as "Mammy".

They did not stand up for the dignity of black women—the backbone of our culture.

Putting political party affiliation aside, Dr. Rice is as much a child of God as President Obama—God has no respect for titles.

What's in a Name?

The "Frederick Douglass Republican" mantra is an inspiration from God. The concept has been test-marketed thoroughly with mind-blowing positive results. Allow me to share two success stories with you.

Success Story #1 - The church I attend is located in an economically depressed, predominately black and heavily Democratic section of Birmingham, Alabama. One morning, I decided to wear one of our trademarked *"Frederick Douglass Republican"* dress shirts to Sunday morning service for the first time. A uniquely powerful design, the phrase *"Frederick Douglass Republican"* was neatly embroidered over the left pocket. The word Republican would be the first thing to grab your attention because it was three times larger than Douglass' name.

Always the agitator, as I entered the building, I was met at the door by Mr. Patterson, an older black gentleman and a staunch liberal Democrat. Of course, the word Republican immediately caught his attention and in a shockingly disgusted voice he asked, *"Smith, are you a Republican?"* *"No sir, I'm a Frederick Douglass Republican"*, was my reply. Mr. Patterson immediately stepped back and threw his hands up saying, *"Oh! Oh! You're a Frederick Douglass Republican!"* *"I can't touch that."*

"Wow! It works!" were my thoughts. This was my opportunity to engage so I seized the moment.

I asked Mr. Patterson, *"Do you believe in the Constitution?"* He said, "yes".

I asked if he would like to keep more of the money he makes. He replied "yes".

"Mr. Patterson," I asked, *"Do you believe life is precious?"* He said "yes".

Finally, I asked if he believed in the biblical teaching if you don't work you should not eat. He replied, "yes".

I said, *"Mr. Patterson you may not be a Republican, but you are definitely a Frederick Douglass Republican. The questions I asked you are the Life-Empowering values of Frederick Douglass."*

He stood there for a moment. Then he replied, *"Smith, you got a point there. I never thought about it like that. A Frederick Douglass Republican! Wow! I'm a Frederick Douglass Republican."*

Success Story #2 - In 2009, while traveling through the Hartsfield-Jackson Atlanta International Airport and sporting one of our trade-marked *"Frederick Douglass Republican*™ polo shirts, a black American college student who inquired about the meaning of the shirt approached me. This gave me an opportunity to engage him and share Douglass' Life-Empowering values.

In about 8-10 minutes, approximately 12 other black Americans surrounded me and listened as I talked. They all voted for President Obama in the 2008 General Election and they all left going away with a totally different outlook—many of them began identifying themselves as a *Frederick Douglass Republican.*

My Prayer

I pray that this book encourages more Americans to become Frederick Douglass Republicans and serves as a rallying call to inspire people to defend our God-given right for self-rule. We will succeed in this endeavor because we stand with the Founding Fathers and on the words of the Almighty God to secure the future of our children and trump the "race card" forever.

> *"As Christians, we should never place race before religion; color before character; a political party before biblical principles; or any president before the PRINCE of PEACE."*

> \- K. CARL SMITH
> The ConservativeMESSENGER™

LIFE-EMPOWERING Value #1:

Respect for the Constitution

"About four years ago I became convinced that it was not necessary to dissolve the union between the states, and that the Constitution of the United States not only does not favor slavery, but it is, in letter and in spirit, an anti-slavery document which demands the abolition of slavery. This radical change in my opinions logically resulted in a change in my actions as well."

- Frederick Douglass,
My Bondage and My Freedom (1855)

Originally, Douglass shared the views of his former mentor, William Lloyd Garrison, denouncing the Constitution as a pro-slavery document in light of the three-fifths clause. He later reversed his opinion after studying the Constitution and analyzing the Founding Fathers' convention notes: Douglass saw the Constitution as having *"noble purposes, which were avowed in its preamble whose words about liberty rendered it an instrument that could be wielded in behalf of emancipation."*[1]

The following bullets are shared with the purpose of equipping us with information to create a healthy dialogue with others about Douglass' views of the Constitution and our God-given right for self-rule:

Douglass' Influence on Dr. King & The Civil Rights Movement

As a result of the previous information, Douglass' positive view of the Constitution influenced Dr. Martin L. King Jr.'s understanding of the "American Dream." King's understanding of the "American Dream" must be seen in light of his concept of the beloved community. Accordingly, King's concept of the "American Dream" was grounded in two sources: *"the American liberal democratic tradition, as defined by the Declaration of Independence and the Constitution, and the biblical tradition of the Old and New Testaments as interpreted by Protestant Liberalism and the black church."*[7] In other words, King was indebted to Douglass for his optimistic thoughts and ideas about the Constitution.

Not only was King indebted to Douglass for his ideas concerning the Constitution, but also he was grateful to Douglass for fighting for the freedom of black Americans. King felt indebted to the Negro leaders of the past, like Frederick Douglass and Booker T. Washington, who paved the way on the racial front, demonstrating that Negroes deserve an equal chance in America.[8]

Douglass on School Choice

Along with his positive view of the Constitution, Douglass' writings express his respect and appreciation for the constitutional principle of educational opportunity through school choice. In other words, every parent has the constitutional right and the God-given right to send their children to the school of their choice. Douglass experienced this issue of "school choice" first-hand when he battled the government for the right to send his nine-year-old daughter, Rosetta, to a better school.

In 1848, the Rochester Board of Education tried to force Douglass to send Rosetta to an inferior segregated Negro school. In his quest to place Rosetta in a quality-learning environment, Douglass sent her to Seward Seminary, one of the best private schools in the area. Upon enrolling in Seward Seminary, Rosetta was promptly expelled because of the color of her skin. Douglass, in righteous indignation and disgust, wrote the following in a letter to the principal: *"I am also glad to inform you that you have not succeeded as you had hoped to do, in depriving my child of the means of a decent education, or the privilege of going to an excellent school. She had not been excluded from Seward Seminary five hours, before she was gladly welcomed into another quite as respectable, and equally Christian to the one from which she was excluded. She now sits in a school among children as pure, and as white as you or yours, and no one is offended. Now I should like to know how much better are you than me, and how much better your children than mine?"*[9]

Douglass desired what every parent wants for their children—the opportunity of receiving a quality education in a safe environment. For this reason, Douglass would be "grievously and shamefully"[10] disappointed in the Obama administration's decision to cut off funding for the D.C. Opportunity Scholarship Program in May 2009.

This scholarship program empowered thousands of poor inner-city children to escape failing public schools in order to attend schools with excellent academics. For Douglass, the best way to get out of slavery or poverty was through a good, quality education.

More specifically, on September 8, 2009, speaking directly to students across the nation, President Obama made the following comment, *"...because you believe, like I do, that all kids deserve a safe environment to study and learn."*[11]

Only a few months prior, the Obama administration passed a $410 billion Omnibus Spending Bill for fiscal year 2009 that cut funding for the D.C. Opportunity Scholarship Program—virtually sending the students back to unsafe, poor-performing schools after the 2010 school year. As a result of public agitation, the Obama administration offered a compromise that will allow current students in the D.C. Opportunity Scholarship Program to continue receiving grants for private school tuition until they graduate from high school. However, this compromise will not permit new students to join the D.C. Opportunity Scholarship Program.

What is even more ironic, President Obama attended private schools and was the recipient of a scholarship. Likewise, his two daughters attend a D.C. private school and 38 percent of the members of Congress have sent a child to a private school.[12]

Every parent—rich or poor, black or white, educated or uneducated—has the constitutional right to send their child to the school of their choice.

The Frederick Douglass Republican Movement is committed to exercising our God-given authority to demand our God-given rights whenever the heavy hand of government threatens our constitutional right to choose the best schools for our children.

LIFE-EMPOWERING Value #2:

Respect for Life

"I oppose slavery in this country, because to expose it is to kill it. Slavery is one of those monsters of darkness to whom the light of truth is death."

- Frederick Douglass,
My Bondage and My Freedom (1855)

Frederick Douglass was a champion for the abolishment of slavery and an unyielding defender of women's rights. The deplorable, degrading, and dehumanizing conditions of slavery—of which he endured himself and witnessed in the lives of others—touched Douglass in such a way that he developed a deep sense of appreciation and respect for human life.

Here are a few excerpts from his writings that eloquently express his respect for human life and his admiration for the human spirit:

- Douglass shared his support for women's rights in the following statement: *"...the subject of what is called 'women's rights' and caused me to be denominated a women's rights man. I am glad to say I have never been ashamed to be thus designated."*[1]

- Douglass expressed his deep admiration on life while being whipped by his master. He wrote: *"When I was treated exceedingly ill; when my back was being scourged daily; when I was whipped*

refused to hate Mr. Auld for his brutal treatment of himself and his family. Instead, Douglass chose to love Mr. Auld without reservation. He expressed his love for Mr. Auld as follows:

> *"In doing this I entertain no malice towards you personally. There is no roof under which you would be more safe than mine, and there is nothing in my house which you might need for your comfort, which I would not readily grant. Indeed, I should esteem it a privilege, to set you an example as to how mankind ought to treat each other."*[13]

For Douglass, the work or ministry of reconciling communities that are separated by race, class and economic status must be grounded in a comprehensive understanding of love. For instance, Martin L. King, Jr.'s "Non-violence Philosophy" was based on a well-rounded interpretation of love.

Like Douglass, King's view of love was expressed in his concept of forgiveness and reconciliation. Forgiveness, according to King, is the loving act on the part of the wronged individual(s) which removes the barriers that inhibit authentic relationships between her/himself and others who have been separated by ignorance, fear, hate and violence.[14] Furthermore, King contended that reconciliation is the result of forgiveness; it is the coming together of disparate parties that have been separated by internal and external barriers that work against wholeness and harmonious relationships between God, people and the world.[15]

For this reason, when confronting opponents, King, like Douglass, did not seek to destroy them, he sought to win their friendship.

The ultimate goal is reconciliation and the outcome of King's non-violent resistance method and Douglass' unconditional love strategy is the creation of the beloved community and a new reality. Douglass used his relationship with Mr. Thomas Auld to produce public awareness and social change. It was love that brought about forgiveness and reconciliation.

Douglass and Nat Turner

America should rejoice in the fact that Douglass responded to the brutality of slavery with love and not hatred. Love is a choice. Douglass chose to love and refused to hate. He could have easily chosen to hate America and hate white people. Instead, he chose to forgive his tormentors.

Douglass could have taken the path of Nat Turner, who led a slave insurrection that murdered more than 57 white people.[16] Rather than have his heart poisoned with the venom of hatred, Douglass forgave those who physically abused him.

Douglass chose to love and Turner chose to hate. Douglass chose non-violence and Turner chose violence. Douglass chose reconciliation and Turner chose recklessness.

Douglass' spiritual strength and historical status positioned him to be the social and political model that will save the soul of our beloved country and re-ignite America's passion for liberty.

Douglass on Immigration

On December 7, 1869 Douglass was asked to address a Boston audience on the question of Chinese immigration. He delivered a speech entitled: "Our Composite Nationality." In this speech, Douglass articulated "why" and "how" immigrants should be received in the United States.

Douglass argued that immigrants are welcomed in the United States because of human rights. He supported Chinese immigration and naturalization—granting them full rights of citizenship, jury duty, voting, and elective office because *there are such things in the world as human rights.*[17]

For Douglass, there is a direct correlation between "human rights" and "inalienable rights"—both are God-given. Douglass contended that human rights supersede racial rights and national rights. Douglass wrote: *"I know of no rights of race superior to the rights of humanity, and when there is a supposed conflict between human and national rights, it is safe to go on the side of humanity."*[18]

After describing "why" America should accept immigrants, Douglass provided his thoughts on the citizenship process for those wanting to settle in the United States. Douglass stated:

> *"We shall mould [shape or form] them all, each after his kind, into Americans; Indian and Celt, Negro and Saxon, Latin and Teuton, Mongolian and Caucasian, Jew and Gentile, all shall here bow to the same law, speak the same*

> *language, support the same government, enjoy the same liberty, vibrate with the same national enthusiasm, and seek the same national ends."*[19]

> Douglass further stated, *"We should welcome to our ample continent all nations, kindreds, tongues and peoples, and as fast as they learn our language and comprehend the duties of citizenship, we should incorporate them into the American body politic. The outspread wings of the American eagle are broad enough to shelter all who are likely to come."*[20]

Notice the process that Douglass advocated. Immigrants should: (1) *Bow to the same law*—respect the rule of law; (2) *Speak the same language*—learn to speak English; and (3) *Support the same government*—become involved in the duties of citizenship.

The first duty of citizenship is to obey the law.

Like Douglass, Frederick Douglass Republicans will not exclude immigrants who want to come to our country for the opportunity to make a better life for themselves and their families. Nonetheless, we insist that they:

1. Obey our laws
2. Learn our language
3. Study and value the importance of our Constitution

LIFE-EMPOWERING Value #3:

Limited Government

"What I ask for the Negro is not benevolence, not pity, not sympathy, but simply justice."

- Frederick Douglass,
My Bondage and My Freedom (1855)

Frederick Douglass believed the role of government is to ensure that every American citizen enjoys the protection of law, his property, his person, his liberty, and the freedom of opportunity—the government's duty is to "protect" us and not to "provide" for us.

The following statements from Douglass further expounds on his perspective of limited government:

Douglass on the Role of Government

+ In highlighting the government's role as protector, Douglass stated: *"The first duty that the National Government owes to its citizens is protection."*[1]

+ In his definition of justice, Douglass outlined the function of government. He maintained: ... *"justice is the perpetual disposition to secure to every man, by due process of law, protection to his person, his property and his political rights. 'Due process of law' has a definite and legal meaning."*[2]

+ Douglass gave his opinion on how the government should deal with the Negro after his emancipation. Douglass stated: *"Let him alone and mind your own business. If you see him plowing in the open field, leveling the forest, at work with a spade, a rake, a hoe, a pick-axe, or a bill -- let him alone; he has a right to work. If you see him on his way to school, with spelling book, geography and arithmetic in his hands -- let him alone. Don't shut the door in his face, nor bolt your gates against him; he has a right to learn -- let him alone. Don't pass laws to degrade him."*[3]

+ Douglass recommended that the federal government refrain from attempting to send the Negro back to Africa. Douglass declared: *"For, until the Negro is respected in America, he need not expect consideration elsewhere. All this native land talk, however, is nonsense. The native land of the American Negro is America. His bones, his muscles, his sinews, are all American. His ancestors for two hundred and seventy years have lived and laboured and died, on American soil, and millions of his posterity have inherited Caucasian blood... I object to the colonization scheme, because it tends to weaken the Negro's hold on one country, while it can give him no rational hope of another."*[4]

Douglass on Entitlement Programs

Douglass encouraged the family members of Negro war veterans to take advantage of the government's Bounty and Pension Laws. Douglass asserted: *"The Government gives to every actual settler, under certain conditions, 160 acres of land. By addressing a letter to the United States Land Office, Washington, D.C., any person will receive full information in regard to this subject. Thousands of white men have settled on these lands with scarcely any money beyond their immediate wants, and in a few years have found themselves the lords of a 160-acre farm. Let us do likewise."*[5]

In the above quote, Douglass offers a perspective on "entitlement programs" that is totally different from how liberal Democrats use government assistance in helping the poor.

Douglass viewed "entitlement programs" as vehicles to elevate the poor (black and white) to become small business owners by land acquisitions and economic business incentives.

In fact, *The Bounty & Pension Laws* of the 1880s were nothing more but "entitlement programs" for the family members of Army and Navy war veterans. These preferential laws created new wealth and enhanced the living conditions of people struggling on the poverty line.

In reality, people with meager resources became "lords of a 160-acre farm"—for many families it ended generational poverty.

This government program created economic incentives for new small-business owners and thereby empowering them to use land to: (1) Produce food; (2) Provide jobs; and (3) Promote other new small businesses.

For Douglass, the best way to create employment opportunities in the private sector was through small-business development.

In 1869, Douglass formulated a land reform proposal that encouraged the federal government to become a purchaser and seller of land in order to counteract the collusion schemes (crony-capitalism, which means passing laws that benefit friends) of southern landowners.[6]

Douglass was not begging for a handout to be given to black Americans, but demanding "fair play" for black Americans.

Douglass' idea of fair play was grounded in the principle of non-exceptionalism. While speaking to an audience of Boston abolitionists in 1862, Douglass declared that fair play means that the ruling majority should: *"do nothing with us, by us, or for us as a particular class... The broadest and bitterest of the black man's misfortunes is the fact that he is everywhere regarded and treated as an exception to the principles and maxims which apply to other men."*[7] Douglass argued that *"we utterly repudiate all invidious distinctions, whether in our favor or against us, and ask only for a fair field and no favor."*[8]

For sure, Douglass viewed land ownership as a viable means for social advancement, economic empowerment, and as an effective tool to level the playing field for all Americans. Douglass wrote:

> *"We must acquire property and educate the hands and hearts and heads of our children whether we are helped or not. Races that fail to do these things die politically and socially, and are only fit to die."*[9]

Douglass on Wealth Redistribution

Douglass did not advocate wealth redistribution but new wealth creation. In his article entitled *The Nature of Slavery* (December 1, 1850), Douglass stated that slavery is built on the distorted philosophy of one reaping the fruits and benefits of another person's hard work and industrious efforts. Douglass wrote, *"…The slave toils that another may reap the fruit; he is industrious that another may live in idleness…"*[10]

Douglass would not support policies that create a WELFARE state, but he would favor laws that produce a WEALTH-FARE economy— starting small businesses to end generational poverty.

Today's entitlement programs must be reformed and restructured so they can transform the poor from being consumers to producers, borrowers to lenders, and poverty dwellers to business owners.

Along with the concept of adding new wealth, Douglass possessed a keen interest in ensuring the government executes the principles of the Constitution so they create and establish an atmosphere of justice and equality for all human beings.

In fact, Douglass served as President Lincoln's conscience. He challenged Lincoln to make the suffering of slaves a priority on his political agenda—pressing President Lincoln to free the slaves. As Moses did with Pharaoh, Douglass carried the cries of his people to the doorstep of the White House. He played a vital role in the making of Lincoln's presidency. He insisted President Lincoln govern by the guidelines of the Constitution.

Douglass' effort was the initial step in advocating civil rights for black Americans.

Douglass on Opportunity

Douglass took advantage of opportunity. As I mentioned previously, Douglass believed the function of government is to protect the freedom of opportunity for its citizens. In sharing his opinion on what to do with the Negro after emancipation, Douglass stated: *"… If you see him on his way to school, with [a] spelling book, geography and arithmetic in his hands – let him alone. Don't shut the door in his face, nor bolt your gates against him; he has a right to learn – let him alone. Don't pass laws to degrade him."*[11] In this statement, Douglass used various metaphors to emphasize the role of government, as it relates to citizens: *"Don't shut the door," "nor bolt your gates,"*–these are metaphors of opportunity.

The function of government is to ensure every American citizen has an opportunity to: (1) Fulfill his or her divine potential; (2) Live with self-dignity, and (3) Exercise his or her God-given rights.

The role of government is not to become the "provider" of our existence, but the "protector" of our existence.

For instance, the welfare system should not become a permanent lifestyle, but it should serve as a temporary boost for a better life.

Living in the midst of horrific slavery conditions, Douglass' optimism and his eagerness to take advantage of an opportunity made him a powerful overcomer. He remained optimistic and confident about his gifts, talents, and skills. More importantly, Douglass was clear about his humanity and his quest for his God-given right for self-rule.

Douglass on Power vs. Rights

The federal government of the United States is so large and powerful that it stands as the most immediate threat to our God-given RIGHTS as American citizens. The government has virtually become the Great Enslaver—a modern-day slave master. Unlike the previous slave system, black Americans are not the only ones being enslaved. It is all of us.

The inverse relationship between the federal government and it's people is based on POWER and RIGHTS. If you analyze the relationship between Master Hugh and Douglass, you will notice there is a never-ending struggle between POWER and RIGHTS—freedom is always under attack.

Master Hugh had POWER and Douglass had no RIGHTS. The federal government has POWER and we as American citizens have RIGHTS. In essence, when the POWER of the slave government increases, our rights decrease. And, when the POWER of the slave government decreases, our rights increase.

Douglass described his inverse relationship with Master Hugh in the following statement:

> *"I was now getting, as I have said, one dollar and fifty cents per day. I contracted for it; I earned it; it was paid to me; it was rightfully my own; yet, upon each returning Saturday night, I was compelled to deliver every cent of that money to Master Hugh. And why? Not because he earned it,--not because he had any hand in earning it,--not because I owed it to him,--nor because he possessed the slightest shadow of a right to it; but solely because he had the power to compel me to give it up."* [12]

Master Hugh permitted Douglass to contract his skills out to other business owners. He was able to earn \$6-\$9 per week and was then required to turn it all over to Master Hugh. In an effort to encourage Douglass to keep up the good work, Master Hugh would sometimes give Douglass six measly cents of his own money—confiscating Douglass' private property.

The slave government has no respect for our private property rights. It uses its POWER to confiscate our earnings before our payroll check is deposited in our banking account.

They do this for basically two reasons: (1) To maintain a firm grip on all aspects of our life; and (2) To confine us to a never-ending slave status.

Our elected officials use their POWER (the power delegated to them by us) to seize our wages as a way to subjugate us. Through incremental tax increases--federal income tax, property tax, sales tax, capital gains tax, estate tax and the possibility of a Valued-Added Tax (VAT)--the slave government is intent on destroying wealth creation in order to shackle and deny us our inalienable right to Life, Liberty, and the Pursuit of Happiness—SELF-RULE.

Considering all levels of government, we pay more in taxes than any other expense category (i.e., medicine, insurance, and fuel). We are all enslaved by incremental tax increases and wealth confiscation.

The Frederick Douglass Republican Movement is committed to re-igniting America's passion for liberty. We will relentlessly hold all elected officials accountable to the noble principles of the Constitution—ensuring the freedom of opportunity and protecting the private property rights of every citizen.

LIFE-EMPOWERING Value #4:

Personal Responsibility

".... And if the Negro cannot stand on his own legs, let him fall also. All I ask is give him a chance to stand on his own legs! Let him alone!... your interference is doing him positive injury."

- Frederick Douglass,
What The Black Man Wants (1865)

Frederick Douglass was a firm believer in personal responsibility. His life is an excellent example of the importance of taking responsibility of one's intellectual growth and educational development.

Douglass was an avid reader. According to the U.S. National Park Services in Washington, D.C., Douglass had over 800 books in his private library. He read all of them and many of them more than once. Those seeking a PhD do not read more than 200 books. In essence, Douglass had the equivalence of four PhDs.

Never having the opportunity of attending one day of formal schooling, Douglass absorbed an enormous amount of information through reading. He developed the ability to grasp information, glean his own conclusions, and stand on his own convictions with confidence and clarity.

In short, Douglass was a critical thinker—an important quality for being responsible for your own life, liberty and pursuit of happiness.

Douglass on Personal Responsibility

A good example of Douglass' analytical thinking skills is found in the way he interpreted the Bible as compared to how his former master, Thomas Auld, interpreted it. His master read the Bible and professed slavery was right. Douglass read the Bible and declared slavery was wrong. In reading the same book, Thomas Auld used the Bible to validate slavery and Douglass used the Bible to denounce slavery.

A free and independent thinker, Douglass offers more thoughts on personal responsibility:

* At the age of six, Douglass desired to run away from slavery, he declared: *"When yet but a child about six years old, I imbibed [received into the mind] the determination to run away...I heard some [of] the old slaves talking of their parents having been stolen from Africa by white men, and were sold here as slaves... Very soon after this, my Aunt Jinny and Uncle Noah ran away... From that time, I resolved that I would some day run away."*[1]

* At age twelve, Douglass enjoyed reading the book: *"The Columbian Orator,"* he wrote: *"I was now about twelve years old, and the thought of being a slave for life began to bear heavily upon my heart. Just about this time, I got hold of a book entitled "The Columbian Orator." Every opportunity I got, I used to read this book. Among much of other interesting matter, I found in it a dialogue between a master and his slave...the conversation resulted in the voluntary emancipation of the slave on the part of the master."*[2]

* At age sixteen, after a victorious two-hour fistfight with his former master, Mr. Covey, Douglass stated: *"This battle with Mr. Covey was the turning-point in my career as a slave... I felt as I never felt before. It was a glorious resurrection, from the tomb of slavery, to the heaven of freedom. My long-crushed spirit rose, cowardice departed, bold defiance took its place; and I now resolved that, however long I might remain a slave in form, the day had passed forever when I could be a slave in fact. I did not hesitate to*

let it be known of me, that the white man who expected to succeed in whipping, must also succeed in killing me."[3]

+ At age nineteen, Douglass, while still enslaved, taught other slaves to read and write. He asserted: *"I held my Sabbath school at the house of a free colored man... I had at one time over forty scholars, and those of the right sort, ardently desiring to learn. They were of all ages, though mostly men and women..., beside my Sabbath school, I devoted three evenings in the week, during the winter, to teaching the slaves at home."* [4]

+ At the age of twenty-one, after running away from slavery, Douglass worked many jobs until he found the one he liked. He claimed: *"I prepared myself to do any kind of work that came to hand. I sawed wood, shoveled coal, dug cellars, moved rubbish from back yards, worked on the wharves [a structure built on the shore], loaded and unloaded vessels, and scoured their cabins. I afterward got steady work at the brass-foundry owned by Mr. Richmond."*[5]

Douglass on Work Ethic

Douglass' work ethic is an impressive example of his spiritual discipline, strength of mind, and physical dexterity. He was a winner. Douglass reached his divine potential because he prepared, studied, trained and applied himself to become the best that God intended for him to be.

His concept of personal accountability led to an impressive and mind-blowing list of major accomplishments: [6]

+ Taught himself to read and write—self-taught homeschooling program;

+ Taught himself to play the violin;

+ Escaped from slavery at age twenty;

+ Delayed his escape from slavery by one year in order to learn how to write as well as read;

- Wrote his first book at age twenty-seven;

- Became the face of the Abolitionist Movement and served as the catalyst within the movement that gave birth to the Republican Party. It was Douglass who declared political war on slavery.

- In 1847, started a newspaper, *The North Star*

- Assisted Harriet Tubman in the Underground Railroad movement through the use of his home in Rochester, NY;

- Became an ordained minister in the AME Zion Church;

- Served as an advisor to five U.S. Presidents (Abraham Lincoln, Ulysses S. Grant, Rutherford Hayes, James A. Garfield and Benjamin Harrison);

- In 1863, served as a recruiter for the Massachusetts 54th Infantry Regiment—volunteered to serve as an officer but was turned down.

- In 1870, became the owner and editor of *The New National Era*, a weekly newspaper in Washington, D.C.

- Without his knowledge, in 1872 Douglass became the first black American to be nominated as a Vice-Presidential candidate— Victoria Woodhull's running mate on the Equal Rights Party ticket.

- Douglass earned $50-$150 per speech during his public speaking career.

Douglass on Welfare

Douglass' idea of personal responsibility is further evidenced by his working relationship with Master Hugh. He rejected the welfare mentality as illustrated in the following statement:

"He would, however, when I made him six dollars, sometimes

give me six cents, to encourage me. It had the opposite effect…
He said if I behaved myself properly, he would take care of
me. Indeed, he advised me to complete thoughtlessness of
the future, and taught me to depend solely upon him for
happiness. He seemed to see fully the pressing necessity of
setting aside my intellectual nature, in order to contentment
in slavery. But in spite of him, and even in spite of myself,
I continued to think, and to think about the injustice of my
enslavement, and the means of escape." [7]

In this quote Douglass informs us that in the life of the slave, the one and only means of existence was the slave master. Likewise, power elite politicians seek to make the government the source of our existence.

For example, today's welfare system is detrimental to the people it claims to care for. In reality, it encourages and bolsters a slave mentality as Douglass describes in his above quote. It creates a perpetual underclass and allows generational poverty to flourish.

Far too many welfare recipients have become solely dependent upon the slave government to care for them—believing the government owes them something—rendering them helpless and unable to escape the slave government's control over their lives. Living on welfare should not become a permanent lifestyle. It should serve as a "jump-start" to a better life.

To be sure, Douglass never turned to his slave master to provide for him—rejected slave master run healthcare. He never embraced a victim mentality or played the race card to gain special consideration. Rather, Douglass developed his gifts and talents and demanded his God-given right for self-rule.

Douglass on Adversity

Douglass' sense of personal responsibility propelled him to become active in the political process. It motivated him to combat ignorance in the educational arena and charged him to confront racism in the form of institutional slavery.

Douglass found fulfillment in tutoring and teaching slaves to read and write on Sundays and during the week, Douglass declared, "*I look back to those Sundays with an amount of pleasure not to be expressed. They were great days to my soul. The work of instructing my dear fellow-slaves was the sweetest engagement with which I was ever blessed."*[8]

Douglass referred to the task of tutoring the slaves as the "sweetest engagement". In other words, he was able to produce a sweet experience in the midst of a stressful situation. Somebody once said that, *"The word STRESSED spelled backwards is the word DESSERTS."* Simply put, every moment of stress is an opportunity for a sweet outcome and a positive experience.

Like Douglass, we must become personally responsible for our own lives and learn to take stressful situations and turn them into sweet experiences, sweet miracles, and sweet memories. If life presents you with a bitter experience, transform it into something sweet.

Whether it's the president, a politician, a preacher or an average citizen—we must use the gift of personal responsibility to lift the most vulnerable in our society.

The Frederick Douglass Republican Movement is committed to re-igniting America's passion for liberty through the power of personal responsibility.

Why I am a Frederick Douglass Republican

I am a Republican, a black dyed in the wool Republican, and I never intend to belong to any other party than the party of freedom and progress.

- Frederick Douglass (1817-1895)

Some people assume incorrectly that the expression, *"Frederick Douglass Republicans™,"* refers to a minority sub-group of the GOP or that it is the name of an organization, a foundation, or a club. Neither is the case. It has nothing to do with racial separation.

The phrase *"Frederick Douglass Republicans"* is an all-inclusive political platform based on the four Life-Empowering Values of Frederick Douglass: (1) Respect for the CONSTITUTION, (2) Respect for LIFE, (3) Belief in LIMITED GOVERNMENT, and (4) Belief in PERSONAL RESPONSIBILITY.

As with the turn-of-phrases, "Tea Party Conservative" and "Reagan Democrat," *"Frederick Douglass Republicans"* is a political point of view and a rallying call to defend liberty.

What began as a mantra has now developed into a nationwide political movement—catching the attention of thousands of Americans—regardless of their race.

Any person may become a Frederick Douglass Republican because it is not about COLOR, it is about VALUES.

eral troops to withdraw from Florida, Louisiana, and South Carolina—officially ending Reconstruction in the South.[12]

First Black State Legislators

As the Republican Party exerted its influence to establish laws and policies that terminated slavery and supported the civil rights of black Americans, the period of Reconstruction (1865-1877) was a time of enormous political progress for black Americans. The first elected black legislators in the Southern states were Republicans. For example:

- In Texas, the first 42 blacks elected to the state legislature were Republicans.[13]

- In Louisiana, the first 95 black state representatives and the first 32 black state senators were Republicans.[14]

- In Alabama, the first 103 blacks elected to the state legislature were Republicans.[15]

- In Mississippi, the first 112 blacks elected to the state legislature were Republicans.[16]

- In South Carolina, the first 190 blacks elected to the state legislature were Republicans.[17]

- In Virginia, the first 46 blacks elected to the state legislature were Republicans.[18]

- In Georgia, the first 41 blacks elected to the state legislature were Republicans.[19]

- In Florida and North Carolina, the first 30 blacks elected to the state legislature were Republicans.[20]

First Black U.S. Congressmen

Along with black Republicans being elected to state offices, they also impacted the political arena on a national level. For instance, the first seven black Americans elected to the U.S. Congress were all Republicans. They were as follows:

Hiram Rhodes Revel from Mississippi was America's first black U.S. Senator. He was an ordained minister in the AME church and served as a chaplain during the Civil War. He was President of Alcorn State University.[21]

Benjamin Turner from Alabama was a slave during the Civil War but within five years after the war he became a wealthy and prosperous businessman. He started a school for black children.[22]

Robert DeLarge from South Carolina was born into slavery. He chaired the Republican Party's Platform Committee and became a state-wide elected official. He died of tuberculosis at the age of thirty-one.[23]

Josiah Walls from Florida was a slave during the Civil War and was forced to fight for the Confederate Army. After being captured by Union troops, he promptly enlisted as a Union soldier and became an officer.[24]

Jefferson Long from Georgia was born a slave. He was self-educated and built a thriving business. He was the first black American to deliver a congressional speech in the U.S. Senate. He served for one session of the 41st Congress (December 1870 – March 1871).[25]

Joseph Hayne Rainey from South Carolina was born into slavery. He served briefly as Speaker of the U. S. House and was in Congress longer than any other black American from that era. Rainey was an advocate of the 1871 Ku Klux Klan Act and the 1875 Civil Rights Act.[26]

Robert Brown Elliot from South Carolina was well educated—he could read in Spanish, French, and Latin. In Congress, he led in the passage of various civil rights bills and later became Speaker of the House in the State legislature. Elliot studied law and established his own practice.[27]

Getting the GOP Back on Track

Today's Republican Party does not resemble the Republican Party of Douglass' day—it has gotten off track by treating the party as a country club and catering to the concerns of the corporate elite.

In fact, both parties have a history of bailing out corporate giants that are labeled as "too big to fail," while overlooking the pain and suffering of the poor and working poor.

In 2009 the Obama administration rescued Wall Street Bankers with a loan of $850 billion. In 2008, the George W. Bush administration supported financial giant Bear Stearns with $30 billion. In 1989,

President George H.W. Bush signed the Financial Institutions Reform Recovery & Enforcement Act, which bailed out the savings & loan institutions in the amount of $293 billion. In 1980, President Jimmy Carter signed the Chrysler Loan Guarantee Act, which provided Chrysler with a loan of $1.5 billion.[28]

If giant corporations are "too big to fail" then the poor and the working poor are "too big to fail".

Both parties—Democrats and Republicans—have failed to adhere to the principles of the Constitution and the values of the Declaration of Independence.

The goal of the Frederick Douglass Republican Movement is to help the modern-day Republican Party recapture its political distinction and become a vanguard of Douglass' four Life-Empowering Values, thereby re-igniting America's passion for liberty.

Making the Poor a Priority

Many are unaware that Frederick Douglass was an ordained minister and his views and concepts about God emanate through his writings. For example, in his letter to his former master, Thomas Auld, Douglass wrote: "...*thanks be to the Most High, who is ever the God of the oppressed.*"[29] Douglass refers to God as the "*God of the oppressed.*" In other words, God stands with and is on the side of people who are being economically, politically and socially exploited. If America claims to be a nation under God and a country grounded in Judeo-Christian principles, then Douglass offers a strong challenge: we must champion the cause of the poor and working poor. In fact, Douglass' motto for his newspaper, *Douglass' Monthly*, was: "Open your mouth, judge righteously, and plead the cause of the poor and needy." - Proverbs 31:9 (NKJV)

We reside in the richest nation in the world but approximately 21 percent of children in the United States live below the poverty line—approximately 16 million children. This includes all children: black, white, brown, red, and yellow. This is more than a race problem; it's a human problem. Along with compassionate prayers and philanthropic gestures, our children need legislative policies that foster education reform and not socialist teaching; self-reliance and not government dependence; and private sector job growth and not the expansion of centralized government.

The goal of the Frederick Douglass Republican Movement is to agitate all political parties to make the pain and plight of the poor and working poor a priority on their political agenda. They must legislate policies that value the most vulnerable in our society and empower the "least of these" in our community—when the "most vulnerable" and the "least of these" are empowered all of us will be elevated.

Facts About the Democratic Party

For the present, the best representative of the slavery party in politics is the Democratic Party.
- Frederick Douglass, *The Slave Party* (1853)

In his books, writings, articles, editorials and speeches Frederick Douglass described the historical events of the Democratic Party that crippled and hindered the liberation of black Americans.

A Deceptive and Deficient Civil Rights Record

+ In 1820, a Democratic-controlled Congress passed the Missouri Compromise, which permitted slavery in the federal territories.[1]

+ In 1850, the Fugitive Slave Law was approved, which required Northerners to return escaped slaves back into slavery or pay a financial fine.[2]

+ In 1854, the Kansas-Nebraska Act was authorized, which extended slavery into Colorado, Montana, Wyoming, Idaho, North Dakota, and South Dakota.[3]

+ In 1857, the Dred Scott Decision was delivered by a Democratic-dominated Supreme Court—it declared that blacks were not persons or citizens but instead were property and therefore have no rights.[4]

+ From 1865 to 1875 Southern Democratic legislatures implemented the following civil rights barriers to prevent blacks from voting and weakened their political representation: poll tax, literary tests, "Grandfather" clauses, "multiple ballots," Black Codes, gerrymandering, white-only primaries, physical intimidation and violence, property ownership requirements, and restrictive eligibility.[5]

+ In 1866, Democrats formed the Ku Klux Klan in order to curtail the political influence of the Republican Party in the black community through intimidation and physical violence.[6]

+ In 1876, a Democrat-governed U.S. House endorsed the Great Compromise. This law ordered federal troops to withdraw from Florida, Louisiana, and South Carolina—officially ending Reconstruction in the South.[7]

+ In 1876, following the withdrawal of the federal troops, the South became known as the "solid Democratic South." As a result, white supremacy was re-established in the South because Democrats controlled southern state legislatures.[8]

+ From 1882 to 1964, 4,743 individuals were lynched—3,446 blacks and 1,297 whites. In fact, during this timeframe the Democrats successfully blocked anti-lynching laws and failed to condemn lynching in its political platforms.[9]

+ In 1896, the Supreme Court—which was controlled by Democrats—issued its *Plessy vs. Ferguson* decision reaffirming its pro-segregation policy.[10]

+ In 1912 Woodrow Wilson, the Democratic candidate for president, promised fairness and justice for blacks if elected. In a letter to a black church official, Wilson wrote, *"Should I become President of the United States they may count upon me for absolute fair dealing for everything by which I could assist in advancing their interests of the race."* But after the election, Wilson changed his tune. He dismissed 15 out of 17 black supervisors who had been previously appointed to federal jobs and replaced them with whites. He also refused to appoint black ambassadors to Haiti and Santa Domingo, posts traditionally awarded to African Americans. Two of Wilson's cabinet ministers, Postmaster General Albert Burelson and Treasury Secretary William McAdoo, both Southerners, issued orders segregating their departments. Throughout the country, blacks were segregated or dismissed from federal positions.[11]

* In 1932, under the administration of President Franklin D. Roosevelt, Democrats placed language in their platform calling for an end to racial discrimination. In spite of this new language Democrats in Congress sought to destroy every piece of civil rights legislation introduced during that time.[12]

* On a positive note, in 1948, President Truman (a Democrat) ended segregation in the armed forces and the civil service through administrative action (executive order) rather than through legislation.[13]

* In 1956, Dr. Martin L. King Jr. and Rev. Ralph D. Abernathy voted for Republican president, Dwight D. Eisenhower.[14]

* Daddy King (father of Dr. Martin L. King, Jr.) and nearly all of the most powerful preachers of the National Baptist Convention were life-long Republicans.[15]

* 1957 Civil Rights Bill – Senate Majority Leader Lyndon B. Johnson deleted from the bill a provision empowering the Justice Department to sue for the enforcement of school desegregation. Both Senator Johnson and Senator John F. Kennedy voted for the jury trial amendment. In its original draft was a condition that certain violations of it could be tried in court without the benefit of a jury trial. This was an important stipulation because

Southern juries would never convict a white person accused of violating the civil rights of a black person.[16]

+ In 1963, Alabama Democratic Governor George Wallace stood at the door of Foster Auditorium at the University of Alabama in a symbolic attempt to block two black students from enrolling at the school.[17]

+ In 1963, Democrat Eugene "Bull" Connor blatantly opposed the Civil Rights Movement by ordering the Birmingham police and firemen to use dogs and high-pressure water hoses against demonstrators.[18]

+ In 1964, Democratic Senators Robert Byrd of West Virginia and Richard Russell of Georgia—through long filibuster speeches— led the fight against the 1964 Civil Rights Act.[19]

The "Slavery Party"

This list of legislative actions and historical events of the Democratic Party is mentioned because it is assumed—especially by the black community—that the Democratic Party has always championed the cause of civil rights for black Americans. Nothing could be farther from the truth. In fact, when it comes to the civil rights of black Americans, the Democratic Party often stood on the side of injustice rather than justice. This is why Frederick Douglass refers to the Democratic Party as the "slavery party"—because their political policies and social actions favored slavery rather than freedom.

Racism has No Political Face

There is no perfect political party. Like the Democratic Party, the Republican Party does not have a clean record as it relates to the liberation of black Americans. For instance, when President Lincoln gave his first inaugural address in 1861, he publicly supported slavery and the Fugitive Slave Law. He stated: *"I have no purpose, directly or indirectly, to interfere with the institution of slavery in the States where it exists. I believe I have no right to do so, and I have no inclination to do so. Those who nominated and elected me did so with full knowledge that I made this and many similar declarations, and had never recanted them."* Douglass was extremely disappointed with the content of President Lincoln's speech and voiced his concerns. Douglass contended, *"It is a double-tongued document...Mr. Lincoln opens his address by announcing his complete loyalty to slavery in the slave States."* [20]

In the beginning of his administration, President Lincoln was more loyal to the slaveholders and to maintaining slavery than to delivering the slaves from oppression. In spite of President Lincoln's unwillingness to end slavery and his lack of support for the civil rights of black Americans, Douglass did not give up on him. He urged President Lincoln to adhere to the noble principles in the Constitution, make the suffering of the slaves a priority on his political agenda, and work toward their emancipation. As a result of Douglass' constant agitation, President Lincoln grew and developed as a leader and later issued the Emancipation Proclamation—liberating the slaves in America.

Racism does not have a political face. Each party has room for improvement. Just as Douglass challenged President Lincoln, the purpose of the Frederick Douglass Republican Movement is to agitate Republican and Democratic politicians who do not adhere to the principles and limitations of the Constitution—passing laws that do not protect our God-given rights for self-dignity and self-rule of all American citizens.

A Christian for Life

As I researched the history of both parties, I was amazed to learn of the Republican Party's impressive record of supporting the liberation of black Americans. Conversely, I was angered to discover the Democratic Party's disgraceful past on civil rights. To put it bluntly, I discovered the history of the Democratic Party has been described in such a way that is not only false, but also politically advantageous.

On the other hand, the Republican Party today does not resemble the Republican Party during Frederick Douglass' life. Therefore, one of the primary objectives of the Frederick Douglass Republican Movement is to help the Republican Party recapture its political distinction through agitation and activism.

I am not an apologist for the Republican Party. I could care less about a party's name. For me, values and principles are more important than party affiliation. That is why I agree with Rep. Robert Brown

Elliot (a black Republican congressman from South Carolina during the Reconstruction Era). He stated:

> *"I am the slave of [Christian] principles; I call no [political] party my master."*

Frederick Douglass'

Success Strategy

"The plan which I adopted, and the one by which I was most successful, was that of making friends of all the little white boys whom I met in the street. As many as I could, I converted into teachers. With their kindly aid,...I finally succeeded in learning to read."

- Frederick Douglass, Narrative of the
Life of Frederick Douglass (1845)

A high achiever in life, Douglass' upbringing was one of suffering, pain, and death—the slave system. His slave experience was worse than the present conditions of urban youth—emotional pains and hardships.

Douglass had no male-presence in the home. He witnessed and was a recipient of physical violence. He saw people succumb to drug abuse. Douglass had no formal schooling, while urban youth attend poor-performing and decrepit schools. He had no healthcare, while urban youth possess inadequate healthcare. He was treated like cattle, while urban youth reside in poverty. Douglass never owned a pair of shoes until the age of eight years, while urban youth wear brand name sneakers as soon as they are able walk.

In spite of these horrendous living conditions, Douglass developed a success strategy that sustained him in slavery and prepared him for freedom. As an ordained AME Zion preacher, Douglass' message of success speaks to the heart and soul of today's urban youth—providing purpose, passion, power and an action plan for their lives.

This chapter will highlight six essential principles that were invaluable to Douglass' powerful success strategy. They are: (1) Listening to the Stories, (2) Savoring the Songs, (3) Becoming an Avid Reader, (4) Courage to Act, (5) Passion for Serving, and (6) Unmatched Work Ethic. Each section will include an inspirational outline based on the Words of God and on the words of Frederick Douglass.

Quality #1: Listening to the Stories:

At the age of six Douglass heard stories from the past and present that fueled his desire to run away from slavery. He declared, *"When yet but a child about six years old, I imbibed [received into the mind] the determination to run away... I heard some [of] the old slaves talking of their parents having been stolen from Africa by white men, and were sold here as slaves... Very soon after this, my Aunt Jinny and Uncle Noah ran away... From that time, I resolved that I would some day run away."*[1]

Karen Gallas, in her book *Why Do We Listen To Stories?*, contends that stories do at least two things to the psyche of children: (1) They help children see the big picture; and (2) They unleash imagination. In Douglass' case, he was able to listen and learn from the stories and then live out the stories that were shared with him by his grandmother.

Understanding stories about the past connected Douglass to the beginnings of his ancestral lineage. In fact, he learned through the power of storytelling that his ancestors were stolen from their African homeland and sold into bondage. Douglass learned that originally his relatives were free people and not slaves. In short, these stories allowed Douglass to understand his present existence as it related to his past.

Along with heeding the stories about the past, Douglass discovered that his Aunt Jinny and Uncle Noah successfully escaped from slavery. For Douglass, this more recent tale of victory and conquest sparked his interest and ignited his inborn passion for liberty. He began to dream of being a free man one day.

Inspirational Outline:
How to Use Stories During Seasons of Stress
   a) **Listen to the Stories . . .**
     [24]*Then he added, "Pay close attention to what you hear.*

The closer you listen, the more understanding you will be given—and you will receive even more.
- Mark 4:24 (NLT)

"I heard some [of] the old slaves talking of their parents having been stolen from Africa by white men, and were sold here as slaves."
- Frederick Douglass, Letter To Thomas Auld (1848)

b) **Learn from the Stories . . .**
[33]*Jesus used many similar stories and illustrations to teach the people as much as they could understand.*
- Mark 4:33 (NLT)

"Very soon after this, my Aunt Jinny and Uncle Noah ran away."
- Frederick Douglass, Letter To Thomas Auld (1848)

c) **Live Out the Stories . . .**
[24]*"Anyone who listens to my teaching and follows it is wise, like a person who builds a house on solid rock.*
- Matthew 7:24 (NIV)

"From that time, I resolved that I would some day run away."
- Frederick Douglass, Letter To Thomas Auld (1848)

Quality #2: Savoring the Songs:
While working for the Auld family as a houseboy in Baltimore, Douglass describes how the slave songs made him feel. Douglass wrote, *"They told a tale of woe which was then altogether beyond my feeble comprehension; they were tones loud, long, and deep; they breathed the prayer and complaint of souls boiling over with the bitterest anguish. Every tone was a testimony against slavery, and a prayer to God for deliverance from chains… To those songs I trace my first glimmering conception of the dehumanizing character of slavery. I can never get rid of that conception. Those songs still follow me, to deepen my hatred of slavery, and quicken my sympathies for my brethren in bonds...Slaves sing most when they are most unhappy. The songs of the slave represent the sorrows of his heart; and he is relieved by them, only*

as an aching heart is relieved by its tears. At least, such is my experience. I have often sung to drown my sorrow, but seldom to express my happiness. Crying for joy, and singing for joy, were alike uncommon to me while in the jaws of slavery."[2]

The slave songs or spirituals were the means by which slaves expressed their desires, disappointments, joys, views of the world, and religious thoughts. Moreover, the slave songs were creatively interwoven with strands of cries, complaints, and celebrations.

Slave songs were not naive depictions of reality and neither were they vague portrayals of their physical existence. They were bold and vivid descriptions of the harsh and cruel injustices of slavery. It is within this social context that slave songs emerged. In fact, the suffering and pain of black Americans produced a collection of music categories: Slave Songs or Spirituals, Negro Spirituals, Gospel, Rhythm & Blues, Blues, Jazz, Hip-Hop, Rap and a host of others. Regardless of the musical forms within the black community, they were birthed by the same experience of pain and suffering.

In a creative way, Douglass used the gift of music to: (1) Survive emotionally, (2) Flourish personally and (3) Plan strategically. He survived emotionally because the slave songs resonate with themes of crying and critiquing. Through the spirituals slaves prayed to God for help and deliverance and they complained to God about the treacherous system of bondage.

In addition, the ability to "cry" and "complain" provided Douglass with the necessary coping skills to handle the emotional stress of slavery.

Douglass flourished personally as well. He focused on mastering the skills of reading, writing, and tutoring. Douglass used the setting of slavery as an opportunity to improve his educational abilities and personal gifts.

Finally, Douglass planned strategically. He designed an action plan that led to his success in living within a society, choosing a career, building relationships, and managing his money wisely.

Solomon was correct when he said, *"Where there is no vision, the people perish"* (Proverbs 29:18 KJV). The opposite is also true: with a vision, people flourish. Douglass' life flourished and prospered because he was captured by a cause and obsessed by a sense of purpose.

Inspirational Outline:
Singing the Lord's Song in a Strange Land?

   a) **Sing to Survive Emotionally . . .**

> [10]*...and those the LORD has rescued will return. They will enter Zion with singing; everlasting joy will crown their heads. Gladness and joy will overtake them, and sorrow and sighing will flee away.*   - Isaiah 35:10 (NIV)

> *"The songs of the slave represent the sorrows of his heart; and he is relieved by them, only as an aching heart is relieved by its tears."*
>   - Frederick Douglass, Narrative of the Life
> of Frederick Douglass (1845)

   b) **Sing to Thrive Personally . . .**

> [17]*To these four young men God gave knowledge and understanding of all kinds of literature and learning. And Daniel could understand visions and dreams of all kinds.*
>   - Daniel 1:17 (NIV)

> *"The mere recurrence to those songs, even now, afflicts me; and while I am writing these lines, an expression of feeling has already found its way down my cheek."*
>   - Frederick Douglass, Narrative of the
> Life of Frederick Douglass (1845)

   c) **Sing to Plan Strategically . . .**

> [11]*"For I know the plans I have for you," declares the LORD, "plans to prosper you and not to harm you, plans to give you hope and a future."*   - Jeremiah 29:11 (NIV)

> *"Those songs still follow me, to deepen my hatred of slavery, and quicken my sympathies for my brethren in bonds...."*
>   - Frederick Douglass, Narrative of the
> Life of Frederick Douglass (1845)

Quality #3: Becoming an Avid Reader:

At age twelve, Douglass enjoyed reading *The Columbian Orator*. He wrote, *"I was now about twelve years old, and the thought of being a slave for life began to bear heavily upon my heart. Just about this time, I got hold of a book entitled "The Columbian Orator." Every opportunity I got, I used to read this book. Among much of other interesting matter, I found in it a dialogue between a master and his slave… the conversation resulted in the voluntary emancipation of the slave on the part of the master."*[3]

Dr. Cornel West, a Princeton University professor, credits reading and education as the positive venue that empowered him to effectively redirect his anger and rage as a young child. Certainly, reading is an excellent way of rechanneling the violent energy and re-routing the rebellious spirit of disgruntled youth. This is what reading did for Douglass during his formative years in slavery. Douglass read for information, inspiration, and innovation.

One book that impacted Douglass' life was *The Columbian Orator*. It contains speeches by George Washington, Benjamin Franklin, John Milton, Julius Caesar, Socrates, Cicero, and others. In reality, this book served as Douglass' mentor. Douglass' mind was shaped and influenced by the information, values, and principles of the orators in the book. *The Columbian Orator*, along with the Holy Bible, equipped Douglass with the internal strength to withstand the external pressures of the slavery experience. In his writings, Douglass referred to *The Columbian Orator* as a "gem" and his "rich treasure." Dr. Lewis V. Baldwin was correct when he stated, *"If we take two children and place them in the same room—one can read and the other can't read—they may be in the same room, but they are in two different worlds."* Even though Douglass was confined to the plantation, he traveled around the world and journeyed through time by way of books. Books possess the power to introduce our minds to a new, exciting world of promises and possibilities.

Douglass read for encouragement. For example, he was greatly inspired by the dialogue between the Master and the Slave in Section 21 of *The Columbian Orator*. As the story goes, the Slave was captured for the second time in his attempt to runaway. As a result, a discussion between the Master and the Slave followed. In the exchange, the Master argued for the support of slavery and the Slave, using impressive debating skills, presented the case for his freedom. Because of the Slave's ability to articulate his point of view, the Master freed the Slave.[4]

In reading this story, Douglass discovered two significant qualities that led to the Slave being set free: (1) Intellect—the Slave was both smart and articulate; and (2) Critical thinking skills—the Slave was awarded his freedom because of his ability to think and draw his own conclusions.

In the words of A.W. Tozer: *"One of the tests of a really fine book is that while you are reading it, you put it down and start to think."* Douglass would have agreed with Tozer. After reading this particular story several times, Douglass was inspired to improve his proficiency in reading and writing. *The Columbian Orator* served as the fuel for his desire to be free. Through the discipline of reading, Douglass became informed, inspired and innovated personally.

Inspirational Outline:
The Power of Reading
   a)   **Read for Information . . .**
      [13]*"When you come, be sure to bring the coat I left with Carpus at Troas. Also bring my books, and especially my papers."*   - 2 Timothy 4:13 (NLT)

      "Just about this time, I got hold of a book entitled 'The Columbian Orator.' Every opportunity I got, I used to read this book."
                      - Frederick Douglass, Narrative of the Life of Frederick Douglass (1845)

      Mark Twain: *"The man who does not read has no advantage over the man who can't read!"*

   b)   **Read for Inspiration . . .**
      [2]*"Write the vision and make it plain on tablets, that he may run who reads it."*   Habakkuk 2:2 (NKJV)

      "…against my learning to read, only served to inspire me with a desire and determination to learn. In learning to read, I owe almost as much to the bitter opposition of my master, as to the kindly aid of my mistress. I acknowledge the benefit of both."
                      - Frederick Douglass, Narrative of the Life of Frederick Douglass (1845)

A Final Word

*"Test yourselves to make sure you are solid in the faith . . .
Give yourselves regular checkups. . . If you fail the test, do
something about it."*

- 2 Corinthians 13:5 (The Message)

Our thoughts produce attitudes resulting in VALUES that are reflected in our behavior. They serve as guiding principles for shaping our worldview and how we live our lives. The way in which we VOTE ought to be the leading indicator of VALUES we possess. Our firmly held beliefs, not our allegiance to a political party, should determine how we VOTE.

Political Values Exercise: Take the time to clarify your political values by completing the following exercise. Don't take this exercise lightly. It cannot be over emphasized that every effort must be made to clarify your political values structure. Freeing yourself from the shackles of political slavery or brainwashing will not come about by accident—it begins with clarifying what issues are important to you.

Taking the time to determine exactly what political issues are important to you can be a difficult task. Establishing your political values will not come about on the spur of the moment so do not try to complete this in one setting. This process requires some serious thought.

Pray about it! Most importantly, be honest with yourself.

Here are some issues you may want to consider in identifying your political values structure. Feel free to use them.

+ Keep taxes low
+ Halt illegal immigration

[16]Gayraud S. Wilmore, **Black Religion and Black Radicalism: An Interpretation of the Religious History of African-American People** (New York: Orbis Books, 1986), p. 70.

[17]Speech texts taken from John W. Blassingame and John R. McKivigan, eds., **The Frederick Douglass Papers, Series One: Speeches, Debates, and Interviews, Vol. 4 (1864-80)** (New Haven: Yale UP, 1991), p. 251-252. For more thoughts on Douglass' ideas on immigration see Greg Moses, "A Neglected Republican Heritage: Frederick Douglass on Immigration and Affirmative Action," Presented at the 2nd National Conference of the Radical Philosophy Association (Purdue) Nov. 17, 1996.

[18]Ibid., p. 252.

[19]Ibid., p. 259.

[20]Ibid., p. 256.

End Notes

Chapter 3
Life-Empowering Value #3:
Belief in Limited Government

[1]Philip S. Foner, ed., **Frederick Douglass: Selections from His Writings** (New York: International Publishers, 1964), p. 702.

[2]Ibid., p. 697.

[3]Ibid., p. 472.

[4]Ibid., p. 768.

[5]Ibid., p. 681.

[6]http://www.heritage.org/research/reports/2011/01/Frederick-douglass-s-america-race-justice-and-the-promise-of-the-founding.Peter C. Myers.

[7]Douglass, "The Future of the Negro People of the Slave States," in Life and Writings, Vol. III, p. 218.

[8]Douglass, "The Color Question," July 5, 1875, in Douglass Papers, Vol. IV, p. 420.

[9]Foner, **Frederick Douglass: Selections from His Writings**, p. 681.

[10]*Narrative of the Life of Frederick Douglass: An American Slave & Other Writings*, p. 144.

[11]Foner, **Frederick Douglass: Selections from His Writings**, p. 472.

[12]**Narrative of the Life of Frederick Douglass: An American Slave & Other Writings**, p. 85.

End Notes

Chapter 6
Facts About the Democratic Party

[1] *Debates and Proceedings in the Congress of the United States*, pp. 2555-2559, 16th Congress, 1st Session, "An act to authorize the people of Missouri Territory to form a constitution and state government," approved March 6, 1820.

[2] PBS online, "Africans in America: The Compromise of 1850 and the Fugitive Slave Act" (at http://www.pbs.org/wgbh/aia/part4/4p2951.html).

[3] *Statues...from December 1, 1851, to March 3, 1855*, Vol. 10, pp. 277-290, 33rd Congress, 1st Session, Chapter 59, May 30, 1854, "An Act to Organize the Territories of Nebraska and Kansas."

[4] *Dred Scott v. Sanford*, 60 U. S. 393 (1856)

[5] David Barton, *The History of Black Voting Rights* (3/2003) (http:www.freerepublic.com/focus/news/1072053/posts.

[6] Smalley, *Brief History of the Republican Party*, pp. 49-50; see also *The Handbook of Texas* online, "Ku Klux Klan" (http://www.tsha.utexas.edu/handbok/online/articles/view/KK/vek2.html).

[7] Seip, *The South Returns to Congress*, pp. 257-258; John R. Lynch, *The Facts of Reconstruction* (New York: Neale Publishing Company, 1913), pp. 171-181; Blaine, *Twenty Years of Congress*, pp. 595-596; Flower, *History of the Republican Party*, p. 333.

[8] Ibid., pp. 171-181.

[9] *University of Missouri-Kansas City* online, statistics provided by the Archives at Tuskegee Institute, "Lynching Statistics by Year" (http://www.law.umkc.edu/faculty/projects/ftrials/shipp/lynchingyear.html).

[10] *Plessy v. Ferguson*, 163 U. S. 537 (1896).

[11] http://trumanlibrary.org/whistlestop/study_collections/desegregation/large/index.php?action=chronology.

[12]Democratic National Committee, "Brief History of the Democratic Party" (athttp://www.democrats.org/about/history.html).

[13]http://pbs.org/wnet/jimcrow/stories_events_segregation.html

[14]Taylor Branch, **Parting The Waters: America in the King Years 1954-1963** (New York: Simon and Schuster, 1988), p. 220.

[15]Ibid., p. 218.

[16]Ibid., pp. 220-222.

[17]Ibid., p. 821-822.

[18]Taylor Branch, **Pillar of Fire: America in the King Years 1963-1965** (New York: Simon and Schuster, 1998), p. 77.

[19]Ibid., pp. 334-336.

[20]Foner, **Frederick Douglass: Selections from His Writings**, p. 433.

Notes:

Notes:

Notes:

Notes:

The Conservative MESSENGER™

TOOLS FOR ENGAGEMENT
"Your Shield" & "Your Sword"

Visit our website to purchase your tools for engagement!

205-492-1810 · www.conservativemessenger.org